D0915002

TOTES PARIS

TOTES PARIS
A Dog's Travel Guide

Rosanne Kang Jovanovski

DOG 'n' BONE

For Totes
My magical unicorn fur baby of rainbows and butterflies.
We will always have Paris.

This edition published in 2020 by Dog 'n' Bone Books
An imprint of Ryland Peters & Small Ltd
20–21 Jockey's Fields   341 E 116th St
London WC1R 4BW   New York, NY 10029

www.rylandpeters.com

10 9 8 7 6 5 4 3 2 1

First published in 2019 by Rosanne Kang Jovanovski
Text and illustrations © Rosanne Kang Jovanovski 2020
Design © Dog 'n' Bone Books 2020

A CIP catalog record for this book is available from the
Library of Congress and the British Library.

ISBN: 978 1 912983 26 1

Printed in China

Design concept and illustrations:
Rosanne Kang Jovanovski

Commissioning editor: Kate Burkett
In-house designer: Maria Georgiou
Art director: Sally Powell
Production controller: Mai-ling Collyer
Publishing manager: Penny Craig
Publisher: Cindy Richards

NOTE: The phonetics provided are
how Totes the Dog would pronounce
the words in French.

TOTES
THE DOG™

Please follow us on ⊙ @totes_the_dog

Contents

Hello!
My name is Totes.

I'm a Shiba Inu.

(shee-bah ee-new)

Shibas originally come from Japan.
"Inu" means dog in Japanese,
but I was born in Nebraska, USA.

My human mommy met me in
New York City—it was love at first
sight. She named me "Totes,"
because she totes me around the
world with her. Together, we've had
many adventures and learned a few
things along the way.

Join me on my travels as
I share with you my favorite people,
places, and things.

Now, let's go to Paris!

Allons-y!

(ah-lon-zee)

Let's go!

Voici Paris

(vuh-ah-see paw-ree)

This is Paris

Paris is one of my favorite cities in the world.
There are countless things to see and do.

Tour Eiffel

(tour ee-fell)

Eiffel Tower

An iron tower built for the
1889 World's Fair. It is so
beautiful, especially when it
is lit up at night.

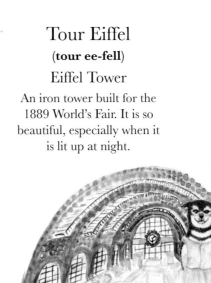

Musée d'Orsay

(moo-zay door-say)

A train station
turned museum.

Pont des Arts
(pone days ah-her)

This "bridge of art" is famous for the thousands of love locks that hung from it. Sadly, the padlocks had to be removed due to their weight, but it's still considered the bridge of love.

Seine
(ssss-n)

This is the river that splits Paris in half. We love taking a boat ride on the Seine at night to see all of its bridges.

Rive Droite
(reave druh-wat)

The right bank, or right side, of the river Seine.

Rive Gauche
(reave go-shhh)

"Gauche" means left. "Rive" means bank or shore of the river. So, this is the left bank of the river Seine.

Arc de Triomphe
(ark duh tree-ohmf)

The biggest arch in the world,
commissioned by Napoleon in 1806.

Champs-Élysées
(shah-mm-zuh eh-lee-zay)

A famous street of cafés,
theaters, and stores.

Place de la Concorde
(puh-lah-ss duh la con-cord)

The largest square in Paris.

Opéra Garnier
(oh-pay-rah gar-knee-yay)

In Paris' oldest opera house, *Le Grand Foyer* (luh grahn foy-yay) ("The Great Hall") is the prettiest in the city.

Le Louvre
(luh loo-vruh)

Once a palace, this is now one of the most famous museums in the world.

Montmartre
(moan mah-trrrr)

The highest point in Paris, this is
a great place to view the city,
to wander, and to buy souvenirs.

Sacré-Coeur
(saw-cray k-her)

The Sacred Heart

A Roman Catholic
church and one of the
city's most iconic
monuments.

Gare du Nord
(gg-argh doo nor)

The station for trains to Northern France and international destinations.

Gare de l'Est
(gg-argh duh lest)

One of the largest of seven train stations in the city.

Place de la République
(plah-ss duh la ray-poo-bleak)

This famous square celebrates the French Republic.

Tour Montparnasse
(tour moan-par-nah-sss)

The only skyscraper in Paris.

Jardin du Luxembourg
(jar-dan doo luxe-ahm-boo-erg)

The Luxembourg Gardens

We love to play here. There are pony rides, sailboats in the fountain, and the most awesome playground for my mini-human friends.

Notre Dame de Paris
(no-trah dah-muh duh paw-ree)

Our Lady of Paris, this is France's prettiest gothic cathedral, which was damaged in a devestating fire in 2019. Restoration is underway.

Marais
(**mah-ray**)

Our favorite
neighborhood
to hang out and
shop in!

Bastille
(**bah-sss-tea-yuh**)

A fortress where, in 1789, the
government was attacked, signaling
the start of the French Revolution.

Opéra Bastille
(**oh-pay-rah bah-sss-tea-yuh**)

Paris' modern opera house.

Une Promenade

(oo-nuh proh-men-ah-duh)

Getting Around

The literal translation is "to walk," but when *une promenade* is paired with another word, like *à vélo* (oo-nuh proh-men-ah-duh ah vay-low) ("to go for a bike ride"), it can convey many ways to get around.

métro
(meh-trow)
subway

taxi
This is the same word in French and English.

❀ Totes' Tip:
Get yourself a *Plan de Paris* (plawn duh paw-ree), a booklet of maps available at any newsstand. It helps me not to get lost and to find lots of hidden parks! *C'est chouette* (seh shoe-het) ("It's great")!

á pied
(ah pee-yay)

on foot or
to walk

Paris is the perfect
walking city, with
many places to sniff.

voiture
(voh-ah-chur)

car

Une promenade en voiture
(oo-nuh proh-men-ah-duh
ahn voh-ah-chur) means
"to go for a drive."

vélo
(**vay-low**)

Bike

Biking is one of my
favorite ways to get
around the city.

En route!
(**ahn-root**)

Let's go!

Totes' Tip:
Grown up humans
can rent a bike almost
anywhere. Look for
the *Vélib* stations.
Génial (jay-knee-al)
("awesome")!

J'adore
mon scoot!
(**jah-door mone scoot**)

I love my scooter!

"Scoot" is a nickname for
a scooter, or small
motorbike.

bus

(boo-sss)

This word is spelled the same as in English, but is prounounced slightly differently. Traveling by bus is a great way to see any city.

Totes' Tip:

Try the double-decker buses where you can hop on and off. Make sure to use the headphones on the bus so you can listen to fun facts while touring.

bateau

(bah-tow)

Boat

Take a nighttime boat ride. The lights on the bridges of Paris and on the Eiffel Tower are simply *magnifique* (mah-knee-feek) ("magnificent")!

Partagez votre selfie!

(par-tah-jay voh-truh selfie)

Share your selfie!

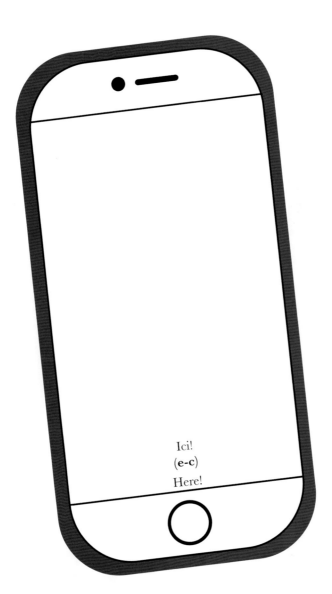

Ici!
(**e-c**)
Here!

Date:
(daht)

Qu'avez vous fait aujourd'hui?

(kah-vay voo fet oh-joo-were-duh-wee)

What did you do today?

_____

_____

_____

_____

_____

_____

_____

_____

_____

Café au lait

Un, Deux, Trois

(uhn, duh, trr-o-ahh)

One, Two, Three

It's important to learn how to count in
a foreign country. Shall we try?

un

(uhn)

one

deux

(duh)

two

trois
(trrr-o-ahh)
three

quatre
(cat-trrrr)
four

cinq
(**sank**)

five

six
(**cease**)

Spelled the same as
in English, but
sounds like "geese"
with an "s."

sept
(**set**)

seven

huit
(**wheat**)
eight

neuf
(**nuff**)
nine
Rhymes with *oeuf* (uh-fff), the French word for "egg."

dix
(**dee-sss**)
ten
Sounds like the French "six" with a "d."

Le Look Parisien

(luh look paw-ree-zee-an)

The Parisian Look

To look French, one must always wear a scarf.
The effortless ways in which Parisians wear them
make them look "insta-chic."

écharpe (**eh-sharp**) or foulard (**foo-lar**)

Both words mean "scarf," but a *foulard* is delicately crafted out of thin,
fine silk or cotton, while an *écharpe* can be made of heavy fabric like
wool. My favorites are found at the classic French artisan
Hermès, La Maison des Carrés (air-mez, la meh-zone day kah-ray), which
translates as "Hermès, the House of the Squares." They come in
many pretty patterns and colors, and are all made by hand!

béret
(brrr-ray)

The beret is a small, round cap classically made of wool. It was first worn by the military and the police, but by the mid-twentieth century it became an emblem of French fashion and art.

marinière
(mah-re-knee-ye-air)

Introduced as the uniform of the French navy, this shirt is also known as a *Breton* (brrr-ehh-tone) as it hails from Brittany—a region in Northwest France. *Les Tricots* (lay tree-koh) *Saint James* have been making the shirt since 1889. It has been *à la mode* (ah la mud) since Coco Chanel included it in her collection and many famous people, like mime artist Marcel Marceau, have worn it.

Totes' Tip:
Not just a scoop of ice cream with your dessert, in French *à la mode* (ah la mud) means "in fashion."

Grand Palais
(grahn paw-lay)

This "Great Palace" is a majestic exhibition hall and museum complex, which houses many events dedicated to art, such as Chanel's fashion shows.

eau de parfum
(oh duh par-fff-um)

This is a perfume with a stronger concentration of fragrance.

eau de toilette
(oh duh twah-let)

Don't worry, it's not toilet water! This is still perfume, but has a lighter scent.

 Totes' Tip:
Perfume was created in ancient Egypt, but the French refined it to how we know it today. Your scent is part of your personal style, and the finishing touch to any outfit.

Nº1
CHIEN
PARIS

PARFUM

Chanel
(shhh-ah-nell)

Mademoiselle Coco Chanel (ma-deh-muah-zel cocoa shhh-ah nell) transformed women's fashion by breaking the rules of what women could wear. After her death, fashion genius Karl Lagerfeld and his beloved cat, *Choupette* (shoe-pet), ran the show for many years, but Mademoiselle Coco will forever be the ultimate muse.

Le Shopping

(luh shopping)

Shopping

Paris is the fashion capital of the world.
I love to shop or simply browse and get inspired.
Here are a few of my most treasured places to visit!

Ladurée

(lah durr-ray)

If you've never tried a macaron you need to come here! Founded in 1862, Ladurée are the makers of the world's most famous macarons. These stunning little pastries are packaged in what look like precious jewelry boxes.

Galerie Lafayette

(gah-lah-ree lah-fah-yet)

Lafayette department store

With one of the finest shoe departments in all of Paris, if you can't find a pair of shoes you like here, well, then you're just too picky!

Les Grands Magasins
(lay grahn mag-ah-zan)

The big stores

Galeries Lafayette and Printemps are Paris' largest department stores.

Printemps
(pran-tahm)

Spring

This store definitely lives up to its name. It carries all of the freshest French looks.

Avenue Montaigne
(ah-ven-oo mon-tine-guh)

and

Rue Saint-Honoré
(roo saint oh-no-ray)

Paris' chicest streets where luxury knows no bounds.

Le Bon Marché
(luh bone mar-shay)

The Good Market

Always on the cutting edge of design and fashion, this department store regularly houses must-see exhibitions.

Poissonnières

(poo-wah-son-ee-air)

Near this metro stop at the top of Paris, search past the stalls of T-shirts and shoes and dive deep within the walls to find the *Marché aux Puces duh Saint-Ouen* (mar-shay oh poo-sss duh sen-wahn), which translates as "The Flea Market of Saint-Ouen." Here you'll discover a labyrinth of antiquities.

Puces de Vanves

(poo-sss duh vahn-vuh)

This flea market at *Porte Vanves* (poor-tuh vahn-vuh) is fantastic. Only open on weekends, you can get everything, from vintage '60s movie posters to fourteenth-century paintings.

Marché des Enfants Rouges

(mar-shay days ahn-fahn roo-juh)

Translated as the "Market of the Red Children," and named in honor of the children from a nearby orphanage who wore red clothes, this charming covered food market is the oldest in Paris.

Merci

(mare-see)

Thank you

This store boasts beautifully curated French housewares, furniture, clothing, and wonderful little jewelry finds that make fun gifts. There's also a great café that houses a gazillion used books. It's a very Parisian place to spend a couple of hours and to fully immerse yourself in all things French. Look for the tiny red car parked out front.

Rue des Francs-Bourgeois
(roo day frahn-boor-juh-wah)

and

Rue Vieille du Temple
(roo vee-yay doo tahm)

Both are ancient thoroughfares of the *Marais* (mah-ray) district, filled with art galleries and beautiful boutiques. Meandering in and out of the stores feels a bit like you're weaving through time in historic Paris.

Milk on the Rocks NYC

So this one's not French, but when my human and I lived in Paris, we used to work at this boutique. I would sit in the window and welcome our clients. It's a great store for kids' clothes and toys. Be sure to pay it a visit!

Date:

(kah-vay voo por-tay oh-joo-were-duh-wee)

What did you wear today?

Montrez-nous votre style!

(mon-tray noo voh-truh steel)

Show us your style!

Dessinez votre look préféré

(day-scene-nay voh-truh look pray-fehr-ray)

Draw your favorite outfit.

Les Musées

(lay moo-zay)

The Museums

With over 100 museums, Paris is a global center of art and culture. Every day, I can find something to inspire me.

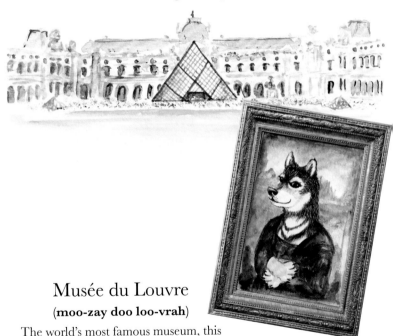

Musée du Louvre

(moo-zay doo loo-vrah)

The world's most famous museum, this palace and fortress houses works from ancient civilizations right up to this century. One of its most treasured paintings is the *Mona Lisa* by Leonardo da Vinci.

Le Centre Pompidou

(luh sahn-truh pom-pee-doo)

This museum features modern and
contemporary art and architecture.

Totes' Tip:

One of my favorite views of Paris is from the rooftop
restaurant George at the *Centre Pompidou.* You can see all
of Paris from there. And, don't miss *La Fontaine Stravinsky*
(la phone-ten straw-vin-ski), the fountain adjacent to the
museum. *C'est trop bien* (seh trow bee-yen) ("It's so good")!

Les musées de Paris sont incroyable!
(lay moo-zay duh Pah-ree sone an-croy-yah-bluh)

The museums of Paris are incredible!

Musée Rodin
(moo-zay ro-dan)

This is a sculpture museum of works by artist Auguste Rodin (oh-goosed row-dan). *Le Penseur* (luh pahn-sur) ("The Thinker") is one of his most notable works.

Fondation Louis Vuitton

**(phone-dah-see-own loo-
wee vwee-tone)**

Established by one of France's oldest luxury
houses, this architectural wonder was
designed by Frank Gehry, and features
modern and contemporary art exhibitions
and concerts.

Le Musée Carnavalet

(luh moo-zay car-nah-vah-lay)

Set in one of the *Marais'* oldest mansions, this
museum is dedicated to the history of Paris.
It houses some personal belongings of
France's last queen, Marie Antoinette
(marie ahn-twah-net).

Musée d'Orsay

(moo-zay door-say)

This is a former railway station that features art from 1848 to 1914.
It has a large collection of art by Edgar Dégas (edgar day-gah),
including *La Petite Danseuse de 14 ans* (la puh-teet dahn-suh-zuh duh
kah-torze ahn) ("The Little Dancer aged 14").

Musée Picasso-Paris

(moo-zay pee-kah-so paw-ree)

This museum is dedicated to the work of Spanish artist Pablo Picasso, well known for his cubist style of painting.

Institut du Monde Arabe

(en-stee-too doo mown-duh ah-rah-buh)

This "Institute of the Arab World" is dedicated to the civilization and spiritual values of Arab culture. It has 240 aperture windows designed by French architect Jean Nouvel (jahn new-vell) that open, close, and control the amount of light and heat entering the building.

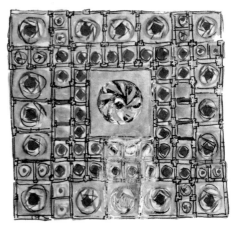

Dessinez votre tableau préféré!

(day-scene-nay voh-truh tah-blow pray-fay-ray)

Draw your favorite painting!

Date:

Qu'avez vous vu aujourd'hui?

(kah-vay voo vew oh-joo-were-duh-wee)

What did you see today?

Artisan Boulangerie

(ar-tea-zahn boo-lawn-jay-ree)

Artisan Bakery

Looking for the best macarons in the city? Or where to pick up freshly handmade madeleines? Paris has no shortage of bakeries to satisfy every sweet tooth.

macaron

(mah-ka-rone)

This is a pastry made from almond flour with a cream center. It comes in many scrumptious flavors and colors. So pretty!

boulanger

(boo-lawn-jay)

This is a baker.

millefeuille

(mill-fffay)

This means "a thousand sheets" since it looks like a thousand sheets of pastry layered with fluffy cream and topped with icing.

pâtissier
(paw-tea-see-yay)

This is a pastry chef.

délicieux!
(day-lee-sssee-yuh)

Delicious!

madeleine
(mah-duh-lane)

This mini sponge cake
is the perfect bite of
vanilla with a hint
of lemon.

Totes' Tip:
My little human friends should always bake
with an adult's help.

Pain et Pâtisserie

(pan eh paw-tea-see-ree)

Bread and Pastries

To say "bread" properly, pinch your nose while you say "pan." Bread and pastry are the basis of any French meal and baking the perfect loaf is an art that has been mastered in France over centuries.

éclair

(eh-cler)

A light pastry covered in chocolate glaze with a cream-filled center.

croissant

(kro-ah-sss-ahn)

The secret to French cuisine is butter. This pastry, named after its crescent shape, is simply buttery, flaky goodness.

pain au chocolat

(pan oh shock-oh-la)

This translates as "chocolate bread"—we know it as a chocolate croissant.

miam!
(mee-yam)

This is the expression for "get in my belly!" Just kidding, it means "yum!"

baguette
(bah-get)

This bread loaf is a national symbol of France. Carry one under your arm and you'll look like a local. It's only fresh for a day, but it's so good, you'll probably eat it right away!

tarte tatin
(tart tah-tan)

Similar to an apple pie, but it's cooked in a skillet and then baked in the oven. Drool!

 Totes' Tip:
If you're looking for a quick bite to eat, find a *boulangerie* and get yourself a baguette sandwich before 2pm. Only go to bakeries marked *Artisan Boulangerie*. They make their bread from scratch—the others don't! It's the best deal in town!

Recette de Gâteau au Chocolat!

(reh-set duh gah-toe oh shock-oh-la)

Recipe for a Chocolate Cake

4 *oeufs* | (uh-fff) | "eggs"

sel | (sell) | "salt"

1^1/$_4$ *bâton* (150g) *de beurre* | (bah-ton duh brrrr) | "stick of butter"

^{1}/$_2$ *cuillère à café du vanille* | (kuh-we-yer ah kah-fay doo vah-knee) | "teaspoon of pure vanilla extract"

^{3}/$_4$ *tasse* (150g) *de sucre brut moulu* | (tass duh soo-cruh bru moolu) | "cup of superfine (caster) sugar"

7oz (200g) *chocolat noir* | (shock-oh-la nuh-war) "bittersweet chocolate"

^{1}/$_3$ *tasse* (50g) *de farine* | (tass der fa-reen) | "cup of all-purpose (plain) flour"

Separate the eggs, putting the whites into a bowl. Add a pinch of salt to the egg white mixture and whip until soft peaks form.

In a separate bowl, mix together the softened butter, vanilla, and sugar.

Melt the chocolate in a third bowl over a pan of boiling water. Add the melted chocolate to the butter, vanilla, and sugar mixure. Then add the egg yolks, one at a time, stirring continuously.

Add the flour to the chocolate mixture, then delicately fold in the egg whites.

Butter and flour one 8-in (20-cm) cake pan, then add the mixture to the pan. Bake for approximately 30 minutes at 350°F/180°C/gas mark 4, or until a toothpick inserted into the center comes out clean.

Totes' Tip:

Remember, dogs can't eat chocolate, so it's best to save the sweets for the humans.

Date:

Quelle est votre recette préferée?

(kell heh voh-truh ray-set pray-fay-ray)

What's your favorite recipe?

Un Petit Café
(uhn peh-teet kah-fey)
A Small Coffee

My human tells me that getting *un petit café* at *le petit café* (luh peh-teet kah-fey) ("small restaurant") is one of life's greatest pleasures. I prefer to simply hang out, dog watch, and discuss the meaning of #doglife.

un petit café
(uhn peh-teet kah-fey)
or
un espresso
(uhn s-presso)
These are short coffees with no milk.

café crème
(kah-fey creh-mmm)
"Coffee cream" is an espresso with equal parts steamed milk.

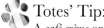 Totes' Tip:
A *café crème* or *café au lait* is usually only ordered in the morning.

café noisette
(kah-fey no-ah-zette)

While *noisette* means "hazelnut," there are no nuts in this coffee. It does, however, have the same nutty color. It's an espresso with some steamed milk.

café américano
(kah-fey ah-mer-ee-kah-no)

As its name suggests, this is the closest to American drip coffee. It's an espresso with more water added to it.

café au lait
(kah-fey oh lay)

Coffee with a cup of hot milk. Always served in a bowl.

chocolat chaud
(shock-oh-la show)

Hot chocolate

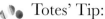

Totes' Tip:
Dogs are allowed in most cafés in Paris. I love *Café de Flore* and *Les Deux Magots*, which are known for the artists, philosophers, and writers that frequented them, such as Simone de Beauvoir and Ernest Hemingway.

Les Deux Magots
(lay duh mah-go)

This roughly translates as "The Two Figurines from the East," which comes from a popular play of the 1800s, and was adopted as the name of the novelty store that first occupied the space.

The dog watching in this neighborhood

C'est top!
(seh top)

It's top notch!

And the human watching isn't bad either.

Café de Flore
(kah-fey duh floor)

One of the oldest coffee houses in Paris, the name comes from "Flora," the goddess of flowers.

brasserie
(brah-sir-ree)

A casual restaurant that offers a large selection of drinks.

restaurant
(ress-tow-rahn)

This is the same as in English. The word originated in France.

bistrot
(bee-strow)

A small restaurant.

Les Essentiels

(lays eh-sahn-see-L)

The Essentials

To speak with a Parisian French accent, I lower my voice, purse my lips, and give my best duck face while I speak. Now it's your turn!

Messieurs-Dames

(messy-er dahm)

This means "ladies and gentlemen." Use this when addressing a group of people.

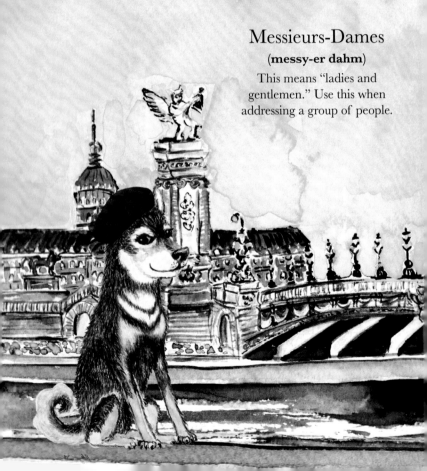

Bonjour madame/monsieur
(bone joo-were mah-dahm/messy-er)
Good day madam/sir

Depending on whom you are greeting, use this as you would "hello."
You would say this before 5pm or dusk, whichever comes first.
For "have a good day," you would say *bonne journée*
(bone-nuh joo-wer-nay).

Bonsoir monsieur/madame
(bone sss-wha-her messy-er/mah-dahm)
Good evening sir/madam

Use this after 5pm or after the sun sets. For "have a good evening,"
you would say *bonne soirée* (bone-nuh sss-wah-ray).

Totes' Tip:
In French culture it's considered polite to
greet someone when first meeting them.
We've found that using one of these magic
phrases helps open the path to friendly
communication and may even get you a
smile for trying to speak French.

Always remember to say please and thank you!

s'il vous plaît
(see voo play)

The direct translation is "if it pleases you" but it means "please."

merci
(mare-see)

Thank you

pardon
(par-doh-n)

Excuse me

oui!
(wee)

Yes

ouais!
(ooo-way)

Yeah

je vous en prie
(juh vooz ahn pre)

This is the more formal way to say
"you are welcome."

de rien
(duh ree-en)

This means "it's nothing," the casual
way to say "you're welcome."

non!
No

Similar to the English pronunciation of
"no," but you have to hold your breath
through your nose, make your lips
round and small, then force the air out.

Où sont les toilettes?
(ew sone lay twah-let)

Where is the bathroom?

Humans always seem to be asking this
question. We dogs have it easier.

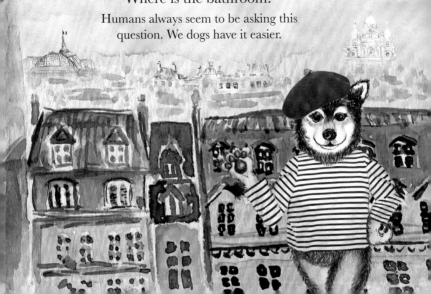

On y va
(own ee vah)

Let's Go

Je m'appelle "Totes!"
(je mah-pell)

My name is Totes!

Bonsoir m_____, trois tickets pour le métro s'il vous plait.

(bone sss-wha-her m_____, trrr-o-ahh tee-keh poor luh may-trow seevoo-play)

Good evening sir/madam, three tickets for the subway please.

Bonsoir m_____, où se trouve la Tour Eiffel ?

(**bone sss-wha-her m_____, ew suh true-vuh la tour ee-fell**)

Good evening sir/madam, where is the Eiffel Tower?

Au revoir

(**oh rev-wah-her**)

Until we meet again.

"Buh-bye!"

Et voilà!

(**eh vuh-wah-la**)

And there you have it!

Merci

(mare-see)

Thanks

We'd like to thank all of our friends who have ever journeyed with and cared for us: Alec, Alliana, Annemarie, Ayami, Christophe, Daniel, Emily, Jo, Karen, Ken, Khairi, Lana, Laura, Lisa, Lulu, Misha, Nelson, Pauline, Samuel, Sarah, Sherise, Stefan, Stephen, Suzanne, and Vicki.

Huge thanks to "Kitty Cat" Franklin, Kathryn E. Shoemaker, Lynn Schnurnberger, Adeena Sussman, Laïka Thomas, Sarah Dale-Harris and Stacey Trimble—your friendship and support on this book are everything.

Special thanks to the guiding lights in my life. Julie, Matthew, and Linda, I am lucky to have you as my siblings. To my special little nuggets: my daughter Aylah, nephew Antonin, and niece Jade whom I love endlessly. Thanks to my parents for teaching me the value of dedication and hard work, and that you must always have a dream.

And to my husband Michael, thank you for the daily lessons in the true meaning of unconditional love, endless patience, encouragement, and support. I love you.

To Totoro "Totes," my muse, my light, and the inspiration for this book, may you rest in peace with Enki, Happy, and Socks. You are forever in my heart.